Wizard of Id Yield

Johnny Hart and Brant Parker

CORONET BOOKS
Hodder and Stoughton

First published 1974 by Fawcett Publications
Inc., New York

Coronet Edition 1976
Fourth impression 1985

Printed and bound in Great Britain for
Hodder and Stoughton Paperbacks, a
division of Hodder and Stoughton Ltd.,
Mill Road, Dunton Green, Sevenoaks,
Kent (Editorial Office: 47 Bedford
Square, London, WC1 3DP) by
Hunt Barnard Printing Ltd,
Aylesbury, Bucks

ISBN 0 340 20776 0

12-14

LOOKS LIKE A BAD CASE OF **GOUT** TO ME.

I'M PUTTING YOU ON A STRICT DIET...

SNAKE EGGS BENEDICT, RATTLESNAKE SOUP, CREAM OF VENOM AND FANG SOUFFLE.

12-16

WHERE'S MY LITTLE PATIENT?

HE'S OUT SUNNING HIMSELF ON A ROCK.

POP

WHAT IS YOUR WISH, O MASTER?

STAY OUT OF MY BOTTLE!

GIVE UP...YOU'RE SURROUNDED!

WE'LL FIGHT TO THE LAST MAN!

WE WANT YOU TOO, CHARLIE!

1-15

1·16

1-29

DON'T YOU DUMMIES KNOW YOU'RE SUPPOSED TO CHALLENGE ANYONE WALKING THROUGH HERE?

SORRY, SHORTY... PUT UP YOUR DUKES!

2-3

THE KING IS A FINK!

2-15

35

3·10

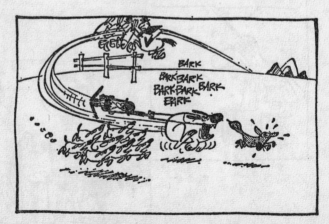

I WOULD LIKE TO PURCHASE A CUSTOM MADE HELMET.

4-14

WITH A NOSE LIKE THAT, YOU HAVE NO CHOICE.

HOW ARE THE PEACE TALKS GOING?

THEY'RE STILL MEETING EVERYDAY.

HOW LONG HAVE THEY BEEN AT IT NOW!?

SEVERAL MONTHS.

4-28

I'LL BET, IF THEY TOOK THOSE GUYS OFF THE EXPENSE ACCOUNT, THEY COULD SETTLE IT TOMORROW.

THERE HE IS... **YEA KING** WHISTLE WHISTLE RAH **CHEER** APPLAUD YELL VIVA STOMP STOMP WHISTLE SCREAM YELL STOMP CHEER SHOUT **HURRAH!** WHISTLE SCREAM

5-6

MY FRIENDS ...I AM AT A **LOSS** FOR WORDS...

IT WORKED, CHARLIE!

5-9

5-12

5-14

LOOK AT THAT GOOFY GREEN ONE, WITH THE BIG NOSE!

WHOOPS

FLOOK

5·15

THERE GOES THE NEIGHBORHOOD.

YOU KNOW...IT'S BEEN QUITE SOME TIME SINCE ANYONE HAS CALLED YOU A FINK.
THAT'S BECAUSE I'VE CLOSED THE CREDIBILITY GAP WITH MY PEOPLE...
... AN INFORMED PEASANT IS A HAPPY PEASANT.
THE KING IS A FINK!
DIRTY TOURIST!
5-26

ALSO AVAILABLE FROM CORONET